The Broad Gauge Railway at Watchet

A Somerset railway station, together with its sidings and the adjacent harbour in the 19th century

Chris Saunders

Contents

Published by LIGHTMOOR PRESS
© Lightmoor Press & Chris Saunders 2016
Designed by Neil Parkhouse

British Library Cataloguing-in-Publication Data. A catalogue record for this book is available from the British Library
ISBN: 9781911038 08 5

LIGHTMOOR PRESS
Unit 144B, Lydney Trading Estate, Harbour Road, Lydney, Gloucestershire GL15 5EJ
www.lightmoor.co.uk
Lightmoor Press is an imprint of Black Dwarf Lightmoor Publications Ltd

Printed in England by Henry Ling Ltd, The Dorset Press, Dorchester
www.henryling.co.uk

Sources and Acknowledgements

The photographs reproduced within these pages are copies from the original plates, most taken over 120 and some over 150 years ago. The number that have survived is perhaps a surprise in today's 'throw away' society and that they have lasted as long as they have shows the value placed on them by the local people of West Somerset and collectors of old photographs. They are a tribute to the photographers' art and the quality of the materials and equipment that they used.

Over a period of many years, photographs have been found by the author in private collections, public archives, on public display and some have been transmitted electronically from private sources. The author wishes to acknowledge the generous assistance of members of the Broad Gauge Society; the archivist of the West Somerset Steam Railway Trust, my friend Ian Coleby; the staff of the Somerset County Record Office (now the Somerset Heritage Centre) and the staff of the Taunton Somerset Studies Library; the members and officers of the Watchet Market House Museum, together with many friends and residents of the town of Watchet.

I especially wish to thank my wife, Mary, for her patience and encouragement over the many years taken to produce this book.

Where possible the image nearest the original negative plate has been used for the best quality of reproduction but some unfortunately have been successively recopied, losing clarity each time. Many prints have also been cropped by successive 'editors' but the fullest image has been used where possible and where quality allows.

The dating of the images has been the most complex part of this project. A process of elimination arrives at the date in the title; however, the author has in some cases offered a more precise date based on educated guesswork. The text indicates the reasoning for the dates.

Author's Introduction

Watchet has always held an attraction for me – and many others judging by the number of visitors each year. As a youngster on holiday in this quaint Somerset town, I used to watch the steam trains passing through between Taunton and Minehead, and the goods engines shunting in the harbour. It was many years later that I discovered that the line had been laid out in Brunel's 'Broad Gauge' and operated with some very strange looking long funnelled engines. As a lifelong railway enthusiast, the history of this line caught my attention. In the 1990s, I started to investigate the early history of Watchet's railway in particular but initial enquires produced copies of just four photographs, from the period around 1870 to 1880.

The concept of such an undertaking only having been recorded four times seemed to be wrong, so I started to delve into the history of the line with little success. Around this time I was introduced to the Broad Gauge Society, whose members either research this subject or produce scale models of the period. The Society's databases held the key to further my research, by leading me to the Public Record Office at Kew (now the National Archives) and the county record offices and their collections.

My collection of images now numbers in the eighties and covers the period commencing just before the arrival of the railway, through to the late Victorian era. The images reproduced here show, not just the railway but also the people of Watchet, at work and leisure. Some of the subject matter has not been seen or recognised before, so as an aid to further research into Victorian railway engineering, I have enlarged some important details.

What was Brunel's broad gauge railway? In September 1835, just after Isambard Kingdom Brunel had been appointed to design and build a railway from London to Bristol, he chose a rail gauge of 7 feet (the extra quarter of an inch came later as a result of easement on curves). Most railways of the time were using the 'standard gauge' of 4 feet $8^1/_2$ inches that the British rail network still uses today. Brunel's reasons for using a unique gauge were based on sound engineering principles rather than on historical inertia.

The wider gauge allowed for greater stability of the trains running on the tracks and greater safety in the event of derailments. Wider stock meant that more could be loaded in the wagons and the passengers had wider compartments in which to sit. There was also the potential for higher speed than the present gauge will allow. If the broad gauge had been adopted as the standard today, then trains could regularly be running at over 200 miles per hour in safety!

I do hope you enjoy these images as much as I have enjoyed finding them and interpreting the subject matter.

Chris Saunders, Highbank, Watchet, 2016

Watchet – The Town

A small harbour town on the north Somerset coast, Watchet had been effectively an isolated seaport for most of its one thousand year history, until the coming of the turnpike road system in the late 1700s. Prior to that, only England's trackways were available for the movement of goods and people. Freight and goods to and from Watchet's harbour were transported inland by pack animals, using the route of Goviers Lane and Liddimore to join the local network of tracks.

There was little need for most people to leave their home town up until this time. However, with the coming of the industrial revolution, there was a need for moving increasing quantities of both goods and manpower. Initially, the stagecoach and the network of turnpikes were able to cope but, with increasing industrial activity, an alternative was required.

Enter the railways. The Great Western Railway was opened gradually from London to Bristol over the period of 1838 to the 1840s, under the guidance of its engineer Isambard Kingdom Brunel. A railway to Watchet, from Taunton, was conceived soon after the main line from Bristol to Exeter was opened in 1844. However, it took a few years of discussions and planning before the West Somerset Railway Act was passed in 1857. This resulted, eventually, in sixteen miles of broad gauge line being opened in March 1862.

The company managed to persuade Isambard Kingdom Brunel to be the engineer to the line. Brunel had visited Watchet in the mid 1850s to survey the area for a proposed new harbour but his plan had been rejected. On his return to the area, he made the preliminary surveys of some possible routes for the railway but, by the time he attended the inaugural meeting of the company, in October 1858, he was very sick and cannot have had much further involvement, although he did supervise the preparation of the initial parliamentary plans, which can be inspected at the Somerset Record Office. Unfortunately, he died before the line was completed, so his assistant, Robert P. Brereton, took over as engineer to the line. The main contractors for the construction were the firm of George Furness, with the sub contractor in charge of these works being Frederick Furniss (no relation). The ceremony of the cutting of the first sod was finally enacted on 7th April 1859.

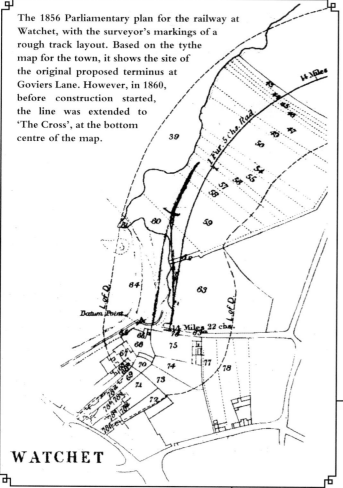

The 1856 Parliamentary plan for the railway at Watchet, with the surveyor's markings of a rough track layout. Based on the tythe map for the town, it shows the site of the original proposed terminus at Goviers Lane. However, in 1860, before construction started, the line was extended to 'The Cross', at the bottom centre of the map.

Even though the gauge had been narrowed, the familiar 'baulk road' permanent way was left in place, the very last section surviving up the line at Crowcombe into the 1930s. Later photographs clearly show baulk road and bridge rail in daily use on the standard gauge well into the 20th century.

A harbour had been in existence at Watchet on the present site, at the mouth of the Washford River, since medieval times. However, constant erosion and battering from storms had caused a series of sea defences to be continually damaged and repaired. In 1861, following the disastrous 'Royal Charter Gale', work commenced to construct the harbour much as we see it today. Spurred on by the imminent arrival of the railway, work advanced apace in co-operation with the builders of the railway earthworks.

This set of images charts the progress of the town's station and harbour from the first days of construction through to the early years of the 20th century, when the last evidence of the broad gauge at Watchet was lost or covered over. The railway and the harbour were clearly seen as of great importance to the local community, as many pictures exist showing some apparently ordinary subject matter by today's standards.

The line was opened in 1862 and soon after, the possibility of an extension to Minehead was mooted but again it took a while to get anything off the ground following the financial crash of 1866; the extension was not opened until 1874.

So now we had twenty-four miles of broad gauge railway, owned by two different companies, the West Somerset Railway and the Minehead Railway but leased to and operated by the Bristol & Exeter Railway. The whole enterprise was eventually absorbed by the Great Western Railway in 1876.

The broad gauge on this line lasted until 28th October 1882, when the familiar gang of navvies undertook the narrowing of the gauge over a weekend of intense activity. This period is sometimes called the Middle Period of the broad gauge but some fine examples of Early Period rolling stock appear in these photographs.

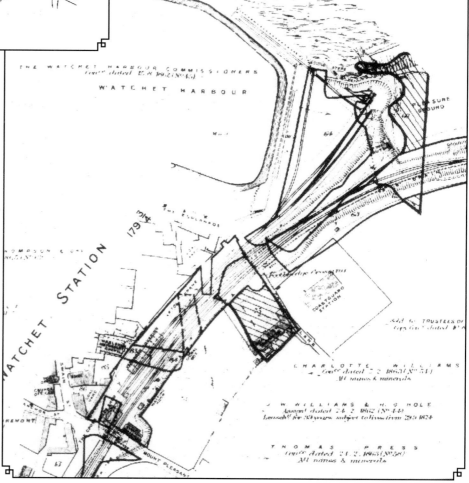

The post broad gauge track layout at Watchet, from the GWR land ownership survey of 1912.

Construction Period
1860 to 1862
This section covers the first known photographs taken in Watchet up to the opening of the railway in spring 1862.

Watchet in the period from the line's inception in the early 1850s is not recorded by photography. The medium was in its infancy at the time and was primarily seen as a mechanical replacement for the portrait painter. However, we are extremely fortunate in that Watchet had among its population several of the pioneers of early topographical photography, beginning from circa 1860 and thus capturing the building of the railway.

James Date, a local businessman, certainly took it up around this time and, fortuitously, he seems to have been retained to record much of the civil engineering activity happening around Watchet at this time. Another photographer, who by coincidence appears in some of Date's pictures, was Daniel Nethercott, who lived a little inland from Watchet. It is unsurprising, given their shared interest, to note that he and James Date were friends.

PLATE 1: WATCHET HARBOUR, CONSTRUCTION OF THE EAST QUAY WALL BY JAMES DATE, JANUARY-FEBRUARY 1861. Looking west from the future site of the turntable, the harbour wall is seen under construction. Planned by the Watchet Harbour Commissioners, work had commenced at Christmas 1860 and this photograph shows early progress on the foundations of the East Quay. They eventually owned only the quay wall and a strip of land 30ft behind it. The railway leased the bulk of the in-filled area behind the quay, which was not used for any serious harbour activity for many years to come. The position of the camera is approximately over the site of the later set of points leading to the turntable. The photographer has managed to get the people of Watchet who feature here to stand still during the lengthy exposure. In the left foreground is a wooden tripod, which forms part of the ropeway delivering mortar to the masons (see PLATE 2 for the other end). Note the pair of wheel sets in the foreground, presumably from one of the contractor's numerous spoil wagons. Around this time the contractor for the harbour works, William Treadwell, suffered industrial action by the men in the photograph. Apparently they went on strike for 'mud money', for having to work in the soft mud between the tides. Having seen the Watchet mud it is surprising that they agreed to work at all! In *Exmoor's Maritime Heritage*, John Gilman incorrectly dates an enlargement from this image as 1856. He describes the ships as of the type that had plied the Bristol Channel coastal trade for decades prior to the 1850s iron ore boom. Seen in this picture are four smacks, a ketch, and a schooner. AUTHOR'S COLLECTION

PLATE 2: MORTAR PRODUCTION ON THE EASTERN ESPLANADE, BY JAMES DATE, JANUARY–FEBRUARY 1861. Looking north-west from what later became Goviers Lane Crossing over the railway, this photograph was taken near to the steps leading to Goviers Lane. It shows the end of the esplanade as it was originally built, as the sea wall, in 1843, with the site of a slipway in the lower foreground. The large millstone on the left was donkey powered and was used to crush calcinated limestone supplied from nearby limekilns. The resulting mortar was carried to the masons by aerial ropeways slung from the tripods. An example of one of these millstones has been preserved and is on display in the Anchor Street public car park. This photograph, together with PLATE NO's 3 and 4, are from the collection of photographic historian Professor John Hannavy. The images are taken from stereographic Ambrotypes, a fairly rare type of photographic medium used in the 1850s and 1860s, usually for portraits. These photographs are not much larger than postage stamps; however, the medium is so good that a great deal of enlargement is possible. The remarkable story behind the discovery of these images was well described by local author, the late Ben Norman, in Volume 30 of the *Exmoor Review* and in a display in Watchet Museum. THE JOHN HANNAVY COLLECTION

PLATE 3: CONSTRUCTION OF THE EARTHWORKS FOR THE RAILWAY TERMINUS, BY JAMES DATE, AUGUST 1861. Looking south-west from Highbank, this picture was taken about 100 yards east of the present Goviers Lane (foot) Crossing. The three onlookers are on the top of the bank where the engine shed was to be built. This spot formed the limit of the original coastline prior to the reclamation works, all the lower ground visible to the right being made up from spoil excavated by the railway. The contractor's wagons and carts can be clearly seen; note that the railway wagons had both standard gauge wheel sets (with outside bearings) and broad gauge (inside bearings); the detail can be studied more clearly in some of the following plates. The pointwork on this temporary standard gauge track is unlikely to have passed a modern safety inspection but shows how a quick connection could be made to an existing track. The building in the background, also seen in PLATE 2, was soon to be demolished, the site being used in the 1870s for the lifeboat house, which is today the Watchet Library. The original plans for the railway allowed for a terminus in the foreground; however, before construction got under way, in May 1860, an Act of Parliament had been passed authorising an extension beyond Goviers Lane to 'The Cross', where the present station is sited. This view shows the excavation of the site of the platform line and the goods yard. The high bank behind the present day platform gives a good indication of how much ground had to be removed at this time. The photographic process, used to obtain the negative, required the use of wet plates, which would have been sensitised in a portable darkroom tent. The amount of equipment involved meant an assistant was needed to help carry this all to site. It appears that James Date enlisted members of his family to help him and then he posed them in some of the photographs. THE JOHN HANNAVY COLLECTION

PLATE 4: CONSTRUCTION OF THE EASTERN ARM, BY JAMES DATE, SEPTEMBER 1861. Looking west from Splash Point, taken from a vantage point long since washed away by the sea. The timber baulk framing was clad with thick timber (as shown in PLATE 20) which was then filled with stones and spoil from the nearby railway cutting. The stone facing in the foreground terminated the pier and acted as a wave break to the adjacent cliff face. On completion of construction, the harbour bed alongside the new wall was dredged to allow ships to lie close to it for loading. In the late 20th century, cargo ships of up to 8,000 tons could use these berths. The curved stone wall in the foreground still remains at the beginning of the 21st century. Note the elm piling adjacent to the cob; many of the stumps of these elm piles can still be seen in the sea bed at some low tides. The short section seen here was all that remained of an extensive system of traditional breakwaters from an earlier period, which offered protection from north-easterly storms. A painting showing these piles can be seen in Watchet Museum. The cob itself was used by the West Somerset Mineral Railway for the dispatch of iron ore to South Wales for smelting. The foreground area, yet to be built up, later became the site of one of the wagon turntables. The large number of ships in the harbour can be appreciated in this and later photographs. At this time, the iron ore boom was in full flow and many of Watchet's ships were engaged in transporting the ore from the West Pier over to the Welsh ports. The white wall facing the photographer was a newly constructed wind break to protect the unloaders from the worst of the wind. THE JOHN HANNAVY COLLECTION

PLATE 5: THE RECENTLY COMPLETED EAST QUAY, WITH CONTRACTOR'S EQUIPMENT, BY JAMES DATE, BETWEEN AUTUMN 1862 AND SPRING 1863. Looking west from Highbank, the quay is still in a very clean state soon after completion; note the broad gauge wagons and the 3-wheeled horse drawn carts, all awaiting disposal by auction sale. The wagons are shown in more detail in an enlargement overleaf. The harbour bottom still shows signs of the recent dredging. On the far left is a wagon turntable, which was installed to provide access to the line running along the quay. However, from photographs it would appear that it was not used, as this siding was blocked with the contractor's wagons, then, after 1867, the tracks here were covered by piles of timber; consequently, it is doubtful if this turntable, unlike the others installed, was ever used for its intended purpose. The two timber track work baulks seen in the bottom left of the picture were still sat here in the 1880s. John Gilman names the nearest ship as *Crystal Bell*, a 94 ton, French-built topsail schooner. There is a thin line crossing the image, which might be a blemish on the plate; alternatively, it could be a telegraph wire, in which case the date would be 1865 or later, however the former is most likely. The photograph was taken from the top of the completed bank near the engine shed, with a 42mm lens; it was probably on a wet collodian plate, using a larger camera than with Date's earlier Ambrotypes. James Date appears to have been retained as official photographer for the construction works. At the end of this period he seems to have invested some of his income in new equipment and possibly a new studio in the grounds of his home in Swain Street. AUTHOR'S COLLECTION

PLATE 5E: THE CONTRACTORS' SPOIL WAGONS. The contractors who built the railway from Taunton to Watchet had no powered mechanical aids to move the spoil around the site. Hand cranes and horse-drawn drags were used, whilst all the excavating was done by hand, with the assistance of some explosives, and the spoil moved by horse and cart or by railway wagons. The rock and spoil removed from the cutting on the approach to Watchet caused many problems, as mixed in with the soft shale and loose stones were layers of very hard limestone. Engineering projects carried out in the vicinity in the late 20th century resorted to using powerful modern explosives to move this type of Watchet rock. The wagons used on this project were popular in the Victorian period. The 4-wheeled carts had an off-centre axle and an open end, allowing easy tipping at the end of each journey. These particular wagons were supplied with two sets of wheels, a narrow set for running on the temporary standard gauge rails and a wide set for running on the finished broad gauge lines. The narrower ones had the wheels set in between the frames, as can be seen in PLATE 3, whilst this enlargement shows the wider set running outside the frames. As an aside, the standard gauge is often referred to as narrow gauge when considered in relation to the broad gauge but this term has been resisted within these pages, as it could cause confusion; many contractors used true narrow gauge systems when building new railways. The wagon on the right has the initials 'GF', presumably those of George Furness, the main contractor. In the background, at the edge of the quay is one of the cast iron bollards used to tie up ships; most of these are still in use some 150 years on.

An engraving showing how this type of contractor's wagon was used by the navvies in 1852.

ABOVE: PLATE 6: FISHERMEN ON THE NEW QUAY, BY JAMES DATE, CIRCA 1862. Looking north-west from the site of the harbour offices, by the look of the abandoned contractor wagons this was taken in 1862 or 1863. An obviously posed photograph, it shows 'fishermen' working on the East Quay and all the structures still look new. The contractor's equipment seems to have been cleaned and made tidy, probably for the auction sale of some of the items remaining after construction. Local records of *The West Somerset Free Press* show that much was sold off immediately the quay and railway were completed, whilst some unsold items were left to decay for years where they had been abandoned (see pictures following). There are at least two broad gauge wagons on the Eastern Pier but as yet no steam cranes, just the two manual derricks. A set of steps were let into the wall, visible just in front of the wagons. The blur on the far right appears to be a horse and cart on its way to the waiting ships. As this is the first photograph of the completed Eastern Pier, it is worth mentioning that the original was constructed with a straight wall, compared with today's cranked design, which is now partially hidden by the 21st century marina walls. Here, also, the bollards used for securing ships to the quay wall are all neatly in a row; by the end of the 20th century, one had become almost buried with concrete, whilst the others still surviving had been badly knocked about. AUTHOR'S COLLECTION

RIGHT: PLATE 7: 'THE CROSS' JUST PRIOR TO THE OPENING OF THE NEW RAILWAY, ANONYMOUS, CIRCA 1861. This is looking north down Swain Street, with the turnpike road in the foreground, just behind the retaining wall and showing the original 'Cross' prior to the railway works. By the surfacing of the road, this was taken sometime before the station was opened in March 1862, possibly in autumn 1861. Some of the families appear to be dressed in their Sunday best for the photograph, which was probably taken by James Date. Many similar compositions have been found, the earliest dated in the 1850s by A.L. Wedlake in *A History of Watchet*. It must be remembered that, at this period, most people were having their photograph taken for the first time. Prior to this, only painting was available to record likenesses which, owing to the cost, was a medium only used by the wealthy. The 1856 map on page 4 shows the road layout here prior to the building of the Minehead Extension in the early 1870s and the diversion of the turnpike. A bedroom window in the house on the left, which still stands today, was used for the photograph taken on the opening day (PLATE 8). Many of Watchet's houses were thatched at this date but some had been re-roofed with slate and a few with Roman type tiles. Although over 150 years have passed since this picture was taken, nearly all the buildings seen here survive and are still recognisable. AUTHOR'S COLLECTION

PLATE 8: THE OPENING DAY, BY JAMES DATE, 31ST MARCH 1862. Taken from a first floor window overlooking 'The Cross', this was the scene on the opening day of the West Somerset Railway. The station has been decorated with greenery and banners, the one over the passenger entrance reading 'WELCOME YE FRIENDS OF PROGRESS'. The temporary decorative fencing and the fir trees were removed soon after the festivities. The station building is constructed of blue limestone blocks (now rendered over in places). Note that the main entrance beyond the donkey cart was identical to that at Williton; however, after the line was extended to Minehead, this entrance gradually fell out of use and it was blocked up in 1894, access then solely being from the door on the platform side of the building. *The West Somerset Free Press* has been a very useful source of reference in compiling captions for these photographs. Many mentions were made of the local constable, John Meeds and it is assumed that the uniformed gentleman who appears in several of these pictures is that very man. Just visible behind the constable's top hat is the equipment for unloading horse-drawn carriages from trains, so that the gentry could continue to their destinations in familiar comfort. Referred to as 'Carriage Chutes', they were mentioned as a feature of Watchet in the railway's advertising. The apparatus consisted of a very stout buffer stop and a hinged iron plate that could be lowered to off-load the carriages from the special trucks used to convey them; just visible behind the foliage is the chute in the raised position. The horses would have been unloaded elsewhere and led along the platform to the forecourt for harnessing to their respective carriages. To the left of the picture is the site of the goods shed, construction of which was not started until after the opening of the line to passengers; it was completed in October 1862. AUTHOR'S COLLECTION

Early Period, Terminus Operations 1862 to 1867

This section covers from the opening of the railway from Taunton until the harbour lines became fully operational.

BRISTOL AND EXETER RAILWAY

Opening of the West Somerset Railway

TAUNTON to WATCHET

On Monday, 31st March, this line will be opened for
PASSENGER TRAFFIC
and the following trains will run:—

DOWN TRAINS

LEAVING			Class 1 & 2 a.m.	Class 1, 2 & 3 p.m.	Class 1 & 2 p.m.	Class 1, 2 & 3 p.m.
Taunton	.	.	9.50	2. 5	5.00	7.30
Bishops Lydeard	.	.	10.5	2.19	5.14	7.44
Crowcombe Heathfield	.	.	10.19	2.33	5.28	7.58
Stogumber	.	.	10.26	2.40	5.35	8. 5
Williton	.	.	10.35	2.49	5.44	8.20
Watchet (arrival)	.	.	10.40	2.55	5.50	8.20

UP TRAINS

Watchet	.	.	8.45	12.30	3.30	6.15
Williton	.	.	8.52	12.36	3.36	6.21
Stogumber	.	.	9. 5	12.49	3.49	6.34
Crowcombe Heathfield	.	.	9.12	12.56	3.56	6.41
Bishops Lydeard	.	.	9.22	1. 5	4. 5	6.50
Taunton (arrival)	.	.	9.35	1.18	4.18	7. 3

This line will open a direct Route to LYNTON, PORLOCK, MINEHEAD, etc., and well regulated coaches will run from Williton in connection with the Expresses and Third Class Trains.

by order of the Directors,

HENRY DYKES,

Superintendent.

Bristol, 19th March, 1862.

PLATE 8A: THE FIRST TIMETABLE. The Bristol & Exeter Railway passenger timetable issued for the opening of the line to the public on 31st March 1862. The goods train workings, which were the main reason for the construction of the line, were given in a separate timetable which was not available to the public. A locomotive was stabled overnight in Watchet engine shed, ready to shunt wagons, and depart at 6.00am for Taunton. Unfortunately, the station at Williton was more conveniently located for stagecoach interchanges, so in the early years Watchet missed out on some lucrative passenger traffic. However, as it was the terminus, it had the unloading ramps for the rail-borne carriages of the gentry to be transferred to road. For those unfamiliar with railway terminology, trains designated as travelling in the Up direction were always those deemed as heading towards London (nominally though this may have been), whilst Down were those trains heading away from London – not up hill and down hill. Sunday services were introduced from May 1862 in response to public demand.

RIGHT: A Bristol & Exeter Railway parcel label, for sticking on packages sent to Watchet.

B & ER

TO

Watchet

PLATE 9: WATCHET FROM CLEEVE HILL, CIRCA 1862. This engraving was a typical pre-picture postcard souvenir, which would have been sold in local gift shops, usually as part of a booklet of such views of the area. The view is from high up on Cleeve Hill, above West Street, with a train leaving for Taunton. The engine shed is clearly visible in front of Sea View Terrace. The date is between 1861 and 1864; the engraving is captioned 'Watchet, Somerset, with the new railway and pier', so it is probably 1862. AUTHOR'S COLLECTION

ABOVE: PLATE 10: WATCHET FROM CLEEVE HILL, ANONYMOUS, CIRCA 1862. This distant view from Cleeve Hill, to the south-west of the town, gives a good indication of the new works associated with the coming of the railways and the boom in the iron ore trade. The new harbour is still pristine and many of the houses are recently built. The West Somerset Mineral Railway's station, which opened in 1855, is the white faced two storey building left of centre, with three or four standard gauge wagons just to be seen in front of it. The newly opened broad gauge line to Taunton can be seen on the right edge of the picture but the 'Beehive' refreshment room has yet to be erected on the Pleasure Ground overlooking the East Quay. Looking from this viewpoint today, the dramatic effects of 150 years of sea erosion are readily apparent. AUTHOR'S COLLECTION

BELOW: PLATE 11: WATCHET FROM ABOVE WEST STREET, ANONYMOUS, CIRCA 1863. This distant view was taken from the area above West Street Beach. On the right is the new engine shed and water tower, whilst the disc & crossbar signal and its attendant policeman's hut can also be seen, above the roof tops left of centre. The banks of the cutting approaching the station are still bare of vegetation, dating this picture to around 1863. The 'Beehive' refreshment room had now been built and can be made out on the far left; between it and the railway signal is another tall post, purpose currently unknown. Slightly to the left of and a little beyond this post, the light coloured stone parapets of Howell's Bridge are visible; this today provides access over the railway to Helwell Bay. The skyline in the distance is the northern end of the Quantock Hills. AUTHOR'S COLLECTION

PLATE 12: WATCHET FROM THE WEST, BY JAMES DATE, CIRCA 1862. This photograph was taken from an area of higher ground north of West Street which coastal erosion has now washed away and shows more clearly the freshly painted engine shed in the right centre background and the water tower in front of it. Just to the right of and beyond the engine shed is the short Seaview Terrace, which still stands today. Two further rows of houses, Almyr Terrace and Portland Terrace, were built on the fields to the right of and behind Seaview Terrace within a few years of this photograph being taken. In the left foreground, there is some construction or repair work underway on the new sea wall between the harbour and West Street Beach, enclosing the area now known as the Mineral Yard; note the gaps in the wall and the ramps down to the beach. The tide is out and several sailing ships can be seen at rest on the mud of the harbour to the left of the London Inn. The traffic generated by the harbour was the primary reason behind the construction of the railway from Taunton. Note the hedge on the left appears to be covered with items of washing left out to dry in the sun, whilst the two men carefully posed by the photographer in the foreground appear to be at rest on the edge of a field of cabbages! AUTHOR'S COLLECTION

PLATE 13: WATCHET TOWN FROM THE BRENDON ROAD, BY JAMES DATE, CIRCA 1862. The newly constructed goods shed, with its glass skylight panels, can be seen to the left of the tree on the right, whilst the station roof can be made out by the base of the trunk. There is no footbridge, as this was built with the Minehead Extension, whilst the turnpike road follows its original winding course down the hill from St. Decumen's Church. On the far side of 'Church Fields', a mountainous heap of timber is stacked in Thorne's timber yard. The foreground shows how wheat was harvested, prior to 20th century mechanisation. This is now the site of the Downfield Hotel development. It would appear that Date had some youthful assistance in carrying his equipment up the steep slope from the town. AUTHOR'S COLLECTION

PLATE 14: THE WESTERN COB, BY JAMES DATE, CIRCA 1862. The Cob, also referred to as the Mineral Quay, with iron ore brought in via the West Somerset Mineral Railway line. This rare view was taken from the timber-built western arm, looking south, late on a summer's day. In the left background is the engine shed again, its paintwork looking clean and bright, and three goods wagons can just be made out on the line to the platform. Just visible, behind the left wagon is one of the policemen's shelters, its position suggesting that it had only just been delivered. The cob was part of the original harbour constructed in the 1700s. During the time span of this series of photographs, it was widened to accommodate buildings for the unloading of iron ore but it is here shown prior to that. It was finally removed in the major reconstruction that followed the storm of 1900. The quality of the facing stonework in the foreground speaks of the pride the masons took in their work. The wagons on the Mineral Quay in the right foreground are part of the fleet of thirty-two owned by the Ebbw Vale Iron Company. They are being unloaded by workmen using a wooden derrick; the one to the left of it is clearly lettered EV 9. The machine obscuring Goviers Lane is a rail-mounted hand crane, useful as it could be moved around as required. AUTHOR'S COLLECTION

PLATE 15: THE EARLIEST KNOWN PHOTOGRAPH OF THE COMPLETED WATCHET TERMINUS AND HARBOUR LINES, ANONYMOUS, CIRCA 1863-64. Taken from the Pleasure Ground, looking south-west, this is in either in the second or third year of the station's operation. The East Quay was still not in general use, owing to an ongoing legal dispute between the railway and the Watchet Harbour Commissioners; however, wagons were run via the turntables on to the Eastern Pier. Goods are being unloaded near the goods shed and some are stored inside the railway fence. A B&ER locomotive can be seen in the platform, presumably waiting to depart to Taunton. Close inspection shows this to be one of the six 4-4-0 saddle

tank engines built by Rothwell & Co. between 1855 and 1856. Note the policeman's shelter at the foot of the signal; this is the first view of the swivel base type used here. The Great Western Railway used this shelter type extensively in the early broad gauge period. The door is facing out to sea, so presumably on this day the policeman was less interested in railway operations than watching the ships. The most well known example of this type of box was located at the western end of Box Tunnel, on the GWR's London to Bristol main line. What appears to be a crack in the plate running diagonally from the top left corner is, on close inspection, a support wire for the signal. To the right of the picture, the esplanade was still boarded off to allow completion of the works. The notice board adjacent to the siding running down to the harbour was probably a warning about the steep gradient; however, the wording is yet to be confirmed. The line from Taunton was usually worked by the Pearson-designed 4-4-0s but tender locomotives are also known to have appeared here. Brunel was aware of the need for good signalling and, in 1841, pioneered the disc & crossbar signal system on the GWR main line; the Bristol & Exeter Railway followed suit. The disc turned towards the line signalled 'All clear', whilst if the crossbar faced oncoming trains, this indicated 'Danger, Stop'. The downward pointing ends to the crossbar indicate that the signal applies to the Down direction (from Taunton). There were many variations of this type of signal but most had similar meanings.

BRISTOL AND EXETER RAILWAY.

WEST SOMERSET BRANCH.

ON SUNDAY, 4th May, 1862, TRAINS will run on this branch, and on EVERY SUNDAY, until further notice.

For full particulars, see Time Bills.

By Order of the Directors,

HENRY DYKES,

28th April, 1862.   *Superintendent.*

PLATE 16: WATCHET TERMINUS AND EAST QUAY, BY JAMES DATE, SUMMER 1864. Taken from the cliff top looking south-west – from about 15ft west of the pillbox on the cliff (now washed away) with a 50mm lens – the contractor's wagons are still in position, now surrounded by two years growth of weeds. The trees are in full leaf and there is a fresh haystack behind the farm wall to the right of the lines. The engine shed is clearly shown, with the enginemen's mess room attached at the front and the water tower in front of that. The small amount of soot that has accumulated over the shed doors testifies to the recent opening of the railway. The water tower is of timber construction and of a standard design; the drawing (page 64) shows the detail of the 6,250 gallons tank. Most branch terminii were equipped with locomotive stabling facilities; that at Watchet could accommodate up to two engines and was necessary because the operation of the line commenced at 6.00am, with an Up goods train to Taunton. The census returns for Watchet in 1871 show a considerable number of railwaymen lodged in the town. Some worked on the Mineral Railway but many others were employed by the Bristol & Exeter and worked on the line to Taunton. As yet, there is no evidence in the picture of the telegraph wires, which were installed in 1865. The short length of the original platform can be seen; this was extended several times and today reaches almost to Goviers Lane. AUTHOR'S COLLECTION

BELOW: PLATE 17: THE DISC & CROSSBAR SIGNAL, BY JAMES DATE, CIRCA 1864. Looking north-west from Highbank, this is the first of a series of six images of the East Quay area that James Date took around this time. Again, the contractors wagons are still very much in evidence but there is no rail traffic to be seen on the quays. In the left foreground is the disc & crossbar signal, with the policeman's hut at its base. Note that on this day the hut has been rotated so that the door looks out on to the railway rather than out to sea. There is a small cut out in the wall of the East Quay, with a set of stone steps, which allowed sailors to climb down to their ships at low tide; in this instance, Date has captured the harbour with the tide in. In the distance, the elm piles protecting the ships at the Mineral Quay can be clearly seen. These were added in 1863-64 to provide added protection from the waves entering the harbour mouth. In the lower foreground, the broad gauge baulk road track shows up well. The transoms are free from ballast and the timbers are visible. AUTHOR'S COLLECTION

ABOVE: PLATE 17E: THE SIGNALLING EQUIPMENT. An enlargement from the previous picture, which more clearly shows several important items of signalling apparatus. The capstan point lever with the target indicator on the top had been invented by Brunel in 1839 and they were commonly found all over the broad gauge system. The idea was to operate and protect facing points on main lines and yard exit points, such as in this case. When the target was visible to the driver, the route was set for the main line but when it was edge on, the line was set for the turnout. The GWR colour scheme was green for the capstan and white for the target. This one appears to have been used for target practice by small boys with stones! An example of this apparatus can be seen at the National Railway Museum and an excellent set of drawings can be found on page 590 of Vol. 1 of *The History of the Great Western Railway*, by E.T. MacDermot (1927). The shelter behind the capstan was provided for the policeman, whose job was to operate the points and signals. This construction included a swivel base to allow the box to be turned, so the occupant was protected from the inclement weather that so often blew in from the Bristol Channel. It appears in several positions throughout this series of photographs.

PLATE 19: LOW TIDE IN THE HARBOUR, BY JAMES DATE, CIRCA 1864. The same wagons and ships appear here as in the right hand portion of Plate 18 above, so possibly it was taken on the same day but the tide has gone out exposing the harbour floor, whilst the pile of sacks and the two men sitting on them have also disappeared. Someone has been making fencing sections, as a stack of them appears on the edge of the work area. The quayside trackwork has still not been used due to the continuing presence of the contractor's wagons and vegetation is starting to take hold. AUTHOR'S COLLECTION

ABOVE: PLATE 18: A PANORAMA OF WATCHET HARBOUR BY JAMES DATE, CIRCA 1864-65. This panoramic view is made up from three photographs found in separate sources by the author. The level of skill involved in accurately maintaining the perspective throughout these three separate exposures speaks volumes about Date's abilities as a photographer – still a very new medium at this time – and also his willingness to experiment. A man can just be discerned sat on the bollard on the left edge of the right hand plate; however, in the original of the centre plate, he has gone, although that fact is not apparent here due to the overlapping involved in lining up the images accurately. Did Date use a megaphone to communicate with the subjects that appear in the pictures or did he just have a very loud voice?

RIGHT SECTION: This section of the panorama illustrates the northern part of the harbour and was taken from the cliff top looking west. Redundant contractor's wagons litter the foreground area and occupy the line along the East Quay. The diamond pattern wagon turntable, which connected the line along the East Quay with that running onto the North Quay, is better shown in the enlargement, RIGHT. Amongst all the sailing ships is a small steam ship with a life belt on the stern – a small foretaste of the forthcoming changes in the maritime coastal trade, which hitherto had been the preserve of sail. AUTHOR'S COLLECTION

CENTRE SECTION: This shows overgrown abandoned contractor's equipment on the East Quay and has been scanned from a photograph of a framed print, so some reflection can be seen from the glass. Regrettably, no better copy has come to light at the current time and the original source is unknown. SOMERSET COUNTY COUNCIL

LEFT SECTION: This shows Watchet terminus, goods yard and engine shed, and may have been taken in 1865, after the installation of the telegraph system. The policeman's shelter has swivelled again to a different aspect, with the door now facing the running lines; the point levers are easy to see, as is the signal lamp at the bottom of the post. The water delivery pipe can be seen on the side of the tank house. The rolling stock in the station area is of great interest, as some of it appears to be of the early B&ER type. Just before the opening of the line to Watchet, the Bristol & Exeter Railway had transferred all its broad gauge stock from the Somerset Central Railway, which ran between Glastonbury and Burnham, to the Taunton area. Most of the stock seen in these early period photographs was already at least eight to ten years old, having been built in the early 1850s. The nearest wagon on the platform road, coupled to a coach, is an open carriage truck; to the author's knowledge, there are no other known photographs of this type of vehicle. Further along, beyond the two carriages, are several iron tilt goods wagons, recognisable by their high curved ends. The majority of those in the yard appear to be B&ER 12-ton coal wagons. Note again the support wire for the signal, whilst there also appears to be steam or smoke issuing from the roof vents of the engine shed. Perhaps the shunting engine had developed a minor problem requiring the use of the shed inspection pit. The shed was transferred to Minehead during the extension works, as it was no longer required here. The foundations were excavated in the 1980s to determine its size and position accurately. The timber lying next to the harbour line is for the construction of a shelter that was shortly to be built here and the telegraph pole next to the platform is very clear to see in this view. In the background, the curving footpath running through Church Fields can be seen, along with the Brendon road to the upper left. AUTHOR'S COLLECTION

PLATE 20: THE NEW HARBOUR, ANONYMOUS, CIRCA 1864. Taken at Splash Point, this posed photograph, thought to be by James Date, appears to be several years after the completion of the harbour works and is one of a series taken on the same day. The somewhat romantic composition illustrates how Watchet and its new harbour was now considered to be a visitor attraction. On the recently completed eastern arm, two broad gauge railway wagons are being loaded by the quayside derricks. Some timber is stacked on the quay awaiting removal. The long wooden breakwater in the background was to last until 1900, whilst the Mineral Quay utilises the earlier cob harbour wall; note the row of elm piles which had been added to give extra protection from the waves. In the centre of the cob, a rake of standard gauge West Somerset Mineral Railway wagons are being unloaded. The cob was widened in 1869 to accommodate increased iron ore traffic and the piles removed. The photograph appears to have been taken on the same day as PLATE 19. The amount of unwieldy photographic equipment needed at that time was heavy to carry about, so photographers of the time tended to make a day of it and capture as many images as possible. AUTHOR'S COLLECTION

PLATE 21: THE WAGON DUMP, BY JAMES DATE, CIRCA 1864. This close up of the contractor's wagons from the harbour lines shows some of the well-ballasted pointwork in the foreground. Close inspection of the picture shows the off-centre positioning of the axles of the wagons, an aid to rapid unloading by tipping from one end. The wagon on its side in the foreground illustrates its width in comparison to its length. Note the young lad (probably Date's assistant) standing in front of the heap of rails, giving a sense of scale. Date positioned himself on the railway close to the large disc & crossbar signal to take this view. AUTHOR'S COLLECTION

PLATE 22: A PADDLE STEAMER EXCURSION, ANONYMOUS, SUMMER 1864. This recently discovered glass plate photograph shows an unidentified paddle steamer calling at the new harbour on an excursion trip. Watchet was not on the regular packet boat routes around the Bristol Channel but was both a destination and a starting point for pleasure trips. A number of excursion vessels were regular visitors here during the 1860s and '70s but one likely candidate for the vessel seen here is *Heather Bell*, a 152 tons iron paddle steamer, built in Glasgow by J.&G. Thompson in 1858, to which this ship bears a strong resemblance; a photograph of her can be found in Grahame Farr's *West Country Passenger Steamers* (1967). She was bought by the Burnham Tidal Harbour Company in April 1864, principally to work on their Burnham-Cardiff ferry service but would also have been used for occasional weekend

and bank holiday excursions. She was sold to Jersey owners in 1867 and broken up at Southampton in 1877. It is not clear whether the passengers, dressed in their mid-Victorian 'Sunday best', are waiting to embark on an excursion setting out from Watchet or are waiting to re-embark, the ship having called here. The two manual derricks on the eastern arm were replaced in 1871 by a single steam crane. Note the pony on the right, grazing amongst the contractor's abandoned wagons. SOMERSET COUNTY COUNCIL

PLATE 22E: THE CONTRACTOR'S WAGONS. A useful enlargement showing the construction detail of the box superstructures of the short wheelbase contractor's wagons. The off-centre axle arrangement is also again clearly shown. In the undergrowth can be seen examples of the frames and wheel sets from damaged wagons. There were also flat top versions for carrying large rocks and stackable materials. Note the wagon in the right background lettered 'GF' for George Furness, the contractor.

Rock & C° London N° 5114.

25. Aug. 1864.

Watchet Harbour, Somersetshire.

LEFT: PLATE 23: ENGRAVING ENTITLED 'WATCHET HARBOUR, SOMERSETSHIRE', BY ROCK & CO., DATED 25TH AUGUST 1864. The view here is from the Pleasure Ground, at a point long ago washed away. The artist has taken liberties with the shipping – the paddle steamer is far too small and would not be in that part of the harbour, whilst no craft would venture to the position occupied by that seen bottom right – but gives a good indication of the new harbour and its surroundings. Beyond the western arm is the sweep of Blue Anchor Bay and in the distance is North Hill, above the town of Minehead. SOMERSET COUNTY ARCHIVE

OPPOSITE PAGE TOP: PLATE 25: THE HARBOUR AND PART OF THE DUMP, BY JAMES DATE, CIRCA 1864. This view, whilst appearing similar to other plates looking down on the abandoned contractor's stock, also includes a B&ER open wagon parked on the East Quay line, a position in which it would have been placed by means of the turntable. It has rounded ends and is painted a relatively dark shade of what is believed to be grey, with its number in white on the right and B&ER on the left. Two more broad gauge wagons can be seen on the eastern arm. This was probably taken on the same day as PLATE 20; note the standard gauge wagon on the Mineral Quay, whilst the ships are in the same positions. AUTHOR'S COLLECTION

PLATE 24: THE WAGON DUMP, BY JAMES DATE, CIRCA 1864. A similar aspect to a couple of previous plates but the clarity of this picture shows much detail of the contractor's tipping wagons and their component parts, whilst on the right, next to the tracks, a point lever can be seen. After completing his contract for building the railway, George Furness won a large contract for the construction of a major section of the Thames Embankment, between Westminster and Waterloo Bridge, which formed a part of London's new sewerage system. Clearly he either did not need these wagons or did not consider it worthwhile transporting them up from Somerset. However, they failed to sell at the auction of surplus equipment following the completion of the line from Taunton and were not finally cleared from site until about 1867. Born in Derbyshire in 1820, Furness had moved to Willesden in 1856 shortly after getting married. In 1882, he completed construction of the Port Victoria Branch on the Isle of Grain. AUTHOR'S COLLECTION

BELOW: PLATE 26: THE SOUTHERN END OF THE DUMP, LOOKING TO THE STATION, BY JAMES DATE, CIRCA 1865. Taken from Splash Point looking south west, the undergrowth has now taken hold on the quay. A goods train is preparing to depart to Taunton from the station. Close inspection of the locomotive shows that it does not seem to be one of the regular 'Pearson Tanks' but instead one of the B&ER's 0-6-0 tender goods engines, of which Stothert & Slaughter built eighteen in three batches between 1849 and 1860; they were designed by Daniel Gooch and, as such, were similar to the goods 0-6-0s he also produced for the GWR. On the bank, next to the locomotive, is a pole for the telegraph system installed in 1865. This was used not only for signalling purposes but also to pass messages for the public. An advertisement in *The West Somerset Free Press* detailed the railway's charges for this service. In the foreground, in the dump, short sections of standard gauge track left from the construction of the line can be seen. Visible in the background is the Brendon Road, part of the turnpike road system replaced by the railway. The WSR minute books in the National Archives, Kew carry lots of detail of the negotiations to move the turnpike in preparation for the Minehead Extension. AUTHOR'S COLLECTION

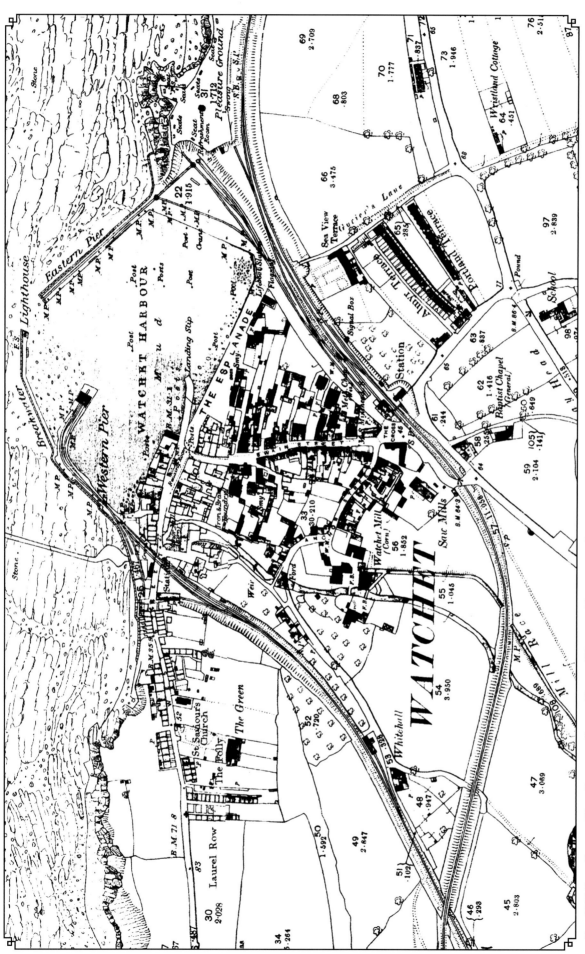

THE 1887 FIRST EDITION 25INS ORDNANCE SURVEY MAP OF WATCHET. The survey of west Somerset was made in 1885-86 and was published in 1887. Prior to this, there were only privately sponsored maps made for landowners, tythe maps and some Admiralty charts for the seafarers. The original survey of the railway had to be made from scratch and a copy is available for inspection in the Somerset County Record Office. This map shows clearly the arrangement of the whole of the harbour. The Western Pier was based on the very much earlier cob wall, which had been in place for many hundreds of years previously. The breakwater to the lighthouse is shown in its wooden period; it was destroyed in a storm in 1900, and subsequently replaced with modern concrete and stone wall which still remains. The Eastern Pier is shown much as it is today but following the 1900 storm repairs, the seaward end was cranked in to provide better protection from the sea, and this predominately wooden structure was also rebuilt in stone. The standard gauge West Somerset Mineral Railway (built between 1855 and 1858) runs on to the western side of the harbour, with its line heading off inland, beneath the line to Minehead and towards the Brendon Hills iron mines which formed its *raison d'etre*, some twelve miles to the south. The company's engine shed can be seen by the house named 'Whitehall', just to the east of the bridge under the Minehead Branch. The ex-broad gauge lines of the latter run onto the eastern side of the harbour and note too, the Pleasure Ground overlooking these to the right, with the refreshment room, swing and even individual seats all marked.

Middle Period
Terminus and Harbour Operations
1867 to 1874

This section covers the period of intense activity on the harbour lines through to the opening of the Minehead Extension in 1874

PLATE 27: THE 'BEEHIVE' ON THE PLEASURE GROUND, ANONYMOUS, BETWEEN 1862 AND 1871. This delightful, if slightly fuzzy shot shows a group of locals in front of the 'Beehive' refreshment room. The figures in the centre foreground have been posed by the photographer and gaze thoughtfully at the ground as they attempt to stand still during the long exposure required. This refreshment room was run by a Miss Date, probably the daughter of the Watchet photographer, who also operated a small café in the town. Regrettably, the 'Beehive' was burnt to the ground some decades later, reported at the time in the local press as being the result of '*Edwardian vandalism*'. The site is now the location of the abandoned 20th century coastguard lookout, currently in use as a mobile phone base station. The raised area in the foreground is the site from which many of the pictures in this volume were taken; PLATE 34 shows this area as seen from the esplanade. The Pleasure Ground was donated to the townsfolk by the Egremont Trustees in the 1860s, the seating and a swing being financed by public subscription. In the background is the engine shed and the disc & crossbar signal, whilst a long row of wagons are visible in the goods yard. COURTESY SOMERSET COUNTY COUNCIL

ABOVE: PLATE 28: THE FIRST COMMERCIAL USE OF THE QUAY, BY JAMES DATE, EARLY 1867. Following the final completion of the legal problems, at the time of this photograph the quay had recently been cleared of the contractor's abandoned equipment and was now in used for timber handling. Note, however, that the track next to the quay was now buried beneath logs and thus apparently still not in regular use. The site had been leased to John Thorne, a local timber merchant, whose lease was subsequently renewed on 28th March 1870. The smoking chimney marking the site of his yard is just visible to the right of the goods shed. In 1867, Watchet was equipped with a gas lighting system, supplied from a gas works in South Road. The new lights can be seen in position but it must have been found that they got in the way of unloading ships, as they disappeared gradually from the quay edge over the years. A chimney can just be glimpsed under construction to the left of Esplanade House; a glance at the next photograph shows it complete. In the distance there is construction work in hand to install the weighbridge used to check the tonnages of the wagons entering and leaving the harbour lines. The very observant will have noticed a disc & crossbar signal in the distance, near the right-hand edge of the picture. This is the stop signal on the standard gauge West Somerset Mineral Railway. This photograph appears to be clearer and with a different contrast to those that have been seen before. Perhaps James Date changed the processing of the plates at this time. AUTHOR'S COLLECTION

BELOW: PLATE 29: WATCHET ESPLANADE AND THE EAST QUAY IN USE, BY JAMES DATE, LATE 1867. In this slightly later photograph, more evidence of John Thorne's timber business can be seen in the foreground. Note the raised saw frame at the bottom left of the picture and also the horse and cart on the muddy harbour floor unloading timber baulks from the sailing ship, which has been identified as a Scandinavian 'snow'. A relatively obscure term nowadays, a snow was a large two masted sailing vessel similar to a brig and is described thus by Young's Nautical Dictionary of 1846: '*A Brig bends her boom-sail (or trysail) to the mainmast, while a Snow bends it to a trysail mast (a third mast much less in diameter, stepped immediately aft of the mainmast): in other respects these two vessels are alike.*' Between it and the quay wall there is a smaller ship with its sail still raised. Around this time, the British construction industry were using large quantities of slow growing Scandinavian pine, which provided long lengths of straight grained timber ideal for the large building projects of the mid Victorian era. Note that the square brick chimney mentioned in the previous caption and situated behind Esplanade House has now been completed. The weighbridge is also now finished and the hut containing the instruments can be seen next to the harbour lines but the quay siding is still covered with timber. Look closely to the right of the goods shed at the site of the Methodist Chapel in Harbour Road and then compare it with PLATE 33. AUTHOR'S COLLECTION

RIGHT AND BELOW: PLATES 30 AND 31: LOADING SACKS OF FLOUR, BY JAMES DATE, CIRCA 1867. These two similar views, from Splash Point, were taken on the same day and together form one of Date's time lapsed stereo pairs (see Appendix 1), although, in the event, it appears that he rejected publishing it. The clue is in the position of the horses and the cart on the quay. In the picture on the right, the horse and cart are parked next to an unloading chute and there is another pile of sacks waiting to be loaded alongside. The carter is sitting on a log presumably waiting for the unloading to be finished. In the second view below, the carter has left his log and is driving the cart away from the (now visible) loading chute but note that the horse standing patiently by the large log has not moved between the two exposures. Some onlookers have also appeared on the esplanade. AUTHOR'S COLLECTION

BELOW: PLATE 32: TWO BOYS ON THE HARBOUR PATH, BY JAMES DATE, CIRCA 1867. This was taken from the same point as the previous two pictures but on a different day, with tree trunks placed where the rails run along the quay. The gas lamp shows up well. The composition of this picture indicates that it was probably taken as a commercial photograph, *i.e.* offered for sale in the form of albumen prints to the general public from local outlets. This site was a favourite of Date's, as it was sheltered from the on-shore winds and the cliff on the right provided a frame for the picture. AUTHOR'S COLLECTION

PLATE 33: A SAILING SHIP UNLOADING TIMBER, BY JAMES DATE, CIRCA 1870. This is another picture 'assembled' from the two halves of a stereo photographic card and shows a twin-masted sailing ship unloading what appear to be sawn timber, quite possibly Scandinavian pine again. Note the horse-drawn 'timber tugs', one loaded and one waiting to be loaded and the stack of smaller logs standing on end, probably to dry out. Unusually, the tide is in for this view but it must have been a calm day as there is no blurring of the ships' masts due to the movement of the waves. Of important note here on the left of the picture is the scaffolding marking the early stages of construction of the Methodist Chapel in Harbour Road. Meanwhile, in the right foreground, a new creosoting tank is also being built. This appears to have been delivered in a number of short sections to be joined up on site and the whole construction is resting on timbers, with further plain sections of tube closer to the camera but partially obscured by some of the wood lying around. Note the sawpit in the centre foreground. The twin images that formed this sterograph were taken with a stereo camera, at the same time. Many of James Date's stereos are time lapsed and thus show movement of the subjects between exposures. See Appendix 1 for the 3D image. AUTHOR'S COLLECTION

PLATE 34: WATCHET EAST QUAY AND SPLASH POINT FROM THE ESPLANADE, BY JAMES DATE, 1870. Taken from outside Esplanade House with a 35mm lens, this view is looking east from the esplanade, in the opposite direction to most of the others, and appears to have been taken on the same day as PLATE 33. Behind the ship is the elevated Pleasure Ground and Miss Date's 'Beehive' refreshment kiosk. The footpath to it from Splash Point is on the left. Note that the policeman's hut is missing from the base of the signal, having been moved to Goviers Lane Crossing. The 1867 gas lights can be seen, as well as the creosote tank under construction. Several horse-drawn timber tugs can just be made out lined up on the quay, and the saw yard shed and the smaller permanent way men's hut can be seen. The large ship is an unidentified French Brig. It is unloading timber either for the local saw mill or more likely for the construction of the Methodist Chapel in Station Road. AUTHOR'S COLLECTION

PLATE 35: WATCHET HARBOUR WITH A SHIP ON THE SLIPWAY, BY JAMES DATE, CIRCA 1867-74. A general view taken from Highbank. Note the clean pointwork in the foreground, which might indicate a date prior to 1874 before the track modifications involved with the Minehead Extension. The points provided access to the engine shed and the turntable, and two of the levers which operated them can be made out. The ship beached on the slipway – an area usually kept clear except in emergencies – might be undergoing a small repair between tides or more likely a quick scrape to remove barnacles. Timber props can be seen preventing the hull from turning right over. Today, vessels in the marina are still beached here for routine maintenance. AUTHOR'S COLLECTION

PLATE 36: BRISTOL & EXETER RAILWAY LOCOMOTIVE No. 74 ON WATCHET TURNTABLE, BY JAMES DATE, SUMMER 1871. This is probably the most well-known photograph of Watchet in broad gauge days, showing B&ER 4-4-0T No. 74 and its crew (as recorded on the reverse of the original print): fireman Frank Bennett (by the cab) and pilotman J. Corbutt (right), with porter W. Windsor looking on. The enginemen wear the white fustian coats and trousers which were popular with footplate crews at this time. Incidentally, Driver J. Coleman was noted as being out of sight on the far side of the engine; he appears in the 1871 census return for Watchet as 'J. Golman', aged 35. The locomotive was built by the Vulcan Foundry in August 1867 and carries its maker's plate on the cabside. After the GWR absorbed the B&ER in 1876, it became GWR No. 2047 and was amongst the last broad gauge locomotives withdrawn in May 1892, following the conversion of the last remaining sections of broad gauge railway to standard gauge. The branch destination disk is mounted on the smokebox door and note the wagons behind – No's 537, 551 and 131 are readable. Also clearly visible is the shiny new creosote tank, whilst the winding gear for the turntable is just in front of the porter. Incidentally, this picture has previously been incorrectly attributed to a later Watchet photographer, Herbert H. Hole, who purchased Date's business in the late 1870s, thus inheriting many of these original plates. AUTHOR'S COLLECTION

PLATE 37: BRISTOL & EXETER RAILWAY LOCOMOTIVE NO. 63 AT WATCHET, BY JAMES DATE, 1869. Clearly showing in the foreground of this view are the stay wires supporting the disc & crossbar signal and there is a wooden derrick in use on the quayside in the centre. Note the construction work on the western sea wall in the left centre background; this was completed in 1869 according to a date stone set in the wall. At the same time, the Mineral Quay was widened in preparation to receive the hydraulic tippers and their buildings, and the new quay wall can be seen rising from the water. This locomotive is one of an older batch of four, built by Beyer, Peacock of Manchester in July 1862; the maker's plate can be seen on the running board, above the front bogie. Note also the white route disc hanging on the smokebox door. The gentleman standing on the tracks is thought to be constable John Meeds, resplendent in his B&ER uniform; his hut at the base of the signal can just be seen behind No. 63's bunker. The large white stone blocks to the right of the engine also appear in several other views. This photograph has also previously been attributed, incorrectly, to H.H. Hole. AUTHOR'S COLLECTION

ABOVE: PLATE 38: THE HARBOUR FROM SPLASH POINT, BY JAMES DATE, CIRCA 1870. Another posed picture, taken from high above Splash Point on a sunny afternoon. Due to the long exposures required with early photography, all pictures involving people had to be posed because they had to stand still for so long. On the right is the first steam crane, which commenced operation in 1870. A bucket hangs from the arm and a second is sat on the quay in front of the crane. This is believed to be the first photograph taken showing the steam crane, which was purchased to help with the increasing level of trade bought to Watchet by the railway. It was delivered with broad gauge wheel sets, making for a very stable machine but it was converted in later years to the less satisfactory, from a stability point of view, standard gauge. A horse and cart are making their way off the eastern arm; the cart appears to be empty, so has presumably just been unloaded and to the left of it is what by this date was the last remaining manual derrick. The large lump of raised ground in the foreground has long since been washed away by the sea and even the path has now been severely reduced in width. On the far side of the harbour, the Mineral Quay can be clearly seen, following its widening in 1869 to accommodate the hydraulic tippers and their buildings, which were still to be completed when this photograph was taken. AUTHOR'S COLLECTION

RIGHT: PLATE 39: THE TURNTABLE AT WATCHET, BY JAMES DATE, 1869. This photograph appears to have been taken on the same day as PLATE 37. The ships are in identical positions but the tide has gone out. The Bristol Channel tides are amongst the highest in the world and the water level at Watchet can change dramatically in minutes. Note the timber decking of the turntable, oil stained and scorched by the heat from engine fireboxes. On the quayside, several carts are unloading what appear to be grain sacks into a ship's hold by means of the sack chute. AUTHOR'S COLLECTION

BELOW: PLATE 40: THE NEW METHODIST CHURCH, BY JAMES DATE, CIRCA 1871. The newly constructed Methodist Church, the main walls built of red brick, with its full height pillars in white stone inlaid with red bricks. The front wall remains to be completed and there are building materials in the foreground. The gap in the wall is now the entrance to the crypt, where the author has given many talks to local societies! The church is still in regular use today and forms part of the West Somerset Methodist circuit. Note the end of a loaded Bristol & Exeter Railway coal wagon standing in the goods yard just coming in to view on the left. The dust from coal being unloaded here would blow everywhere in strong winds, a problem that persisted right to the very end of rail-borne deliveries in the 1960s. AUTHOR'S COLLECTION

ABOVE: PLATE 40E: AN ENLARGEMENT OF THE BRISTOL & EXETER RAILWAY COAL WAGON. An historically valuable image, showing the construction of this B&ER 12-ton coal wagon. Many details of the mid-Victorian design are shown. At this time the body and under frame were built primarily of timber, whilst the body sides were made up of three thick planks held together by stout framing. The coupling and safety back up chains show well, as does the iron loop on the sole bar, where horse chains were connected for shunting. The axlebox is mounted beneath a very short leaf spring. The 4ft diameter split 10-spoke wheels projected up into the load space and were protected by boxes on the floor of the wagon. There were no brakes on this type of wagon, so careful shunting with a horse would have been needed on the gradient down to the quay. The numbers 4.1.2 indicate an unladen weight of 4 tons, 1 hundredweight and 2 quarters or, in modern day terms, about 5,000 kilos. AUTHOR'S COLLECTION

PLATE 41: EMPTY WAGONS ON THE HARBOUR LINES, BY JAMES DATE, SUMMER 1871. In the foreground is the recently completed quay workers' shelter and beyond it are two contractors' wagons, one of which looks quite new. In the left middle distance, the nearest wagon parked on the goods loop appears to be a brake van. A selection of B&ER open wagons feature in the right foreground and details regarding them are given with the enlargement which follows on page 39. On the left, just below the water tank, are two target type point levers. The shelter protecting Goviers Lane Crossing may have been the one beneath the signal, probably moved in order that the policeman was on hand to guide the public over the crossing. The gradients, from the running line down to the yard and down from there to the harbour, are well shown in this view. On 4th October 1862, James Curry, a supernumerary porter, was fatally injured when riding a wagon down these slopes. He was standing on an axlebox when he slipped and his leg was caught between the rotating spokes of the wheel and the frame; he died later that day from his injuries. Another accident was reported in September 1874, when John Saunders, the 13-year old son of a guard on the B&ER, lost a leg while playing on wagons on the harbour lines. He caught his toe under a wheel and then his right leg was caught in the spokes before the horse pulling them could be stopped. AUTHOR'S COLLECTION

LEFT: PLATE 42: 'THE TRAIN SPOTTERS', BY JAMES DATE, POST 1871. Sitting on the fence overlooking the railway, these three boys would have had a fine view of the goings on in the station and goods yard below. Some wagons are in the siding, including a loaded and sheeted iron tilt wagon. In front of the boys is the roof of a passenger coach which, by the spacing of the roof mounted oil lamps, is a 4-compartment First Class carriage. A petrol station was built on this grassed area in the mid 20th century but the site now forms the rear gardens of houses built in the 1990s. AUTHOR'S COLLECTION

OPPOSITE PAGE TOP: PLATE 41E: EMPTY BROAD GAUGE OPEN WAGONS: This detail enlargement from the plate on page 37 shows the interiors of a number of empty broad gauge open wagons and is of great use to researchers of early railway design, with a number of variations shown here. Nearest is a 4-plank wagon with drop doors and straight top ends, whilst the next is a typical 5-plank type, with a continuous top plank preventing the wagon body from distorting when fully loaded. The third is another 4-plank but has the rounded top to the ends. This one seems to be a standard B&ER 12-ton coal wagon and inside it, one of the projecting boxes covering the wheels can be clearly seen. The fifth wagon has only one rounded end – it is thought that these were designed to run in pairs to carry longer loads – and flanking it are two more 4-plank opens with straight ends. The final wagon appears to be a 3-plank open. Note, too, the thick planks on the right, products of the saw pit.

RIGHT: PLATE 43: TIMBER AND COAL WAGONS ON THE EAST QUAY, BY JAMES DATE, CIRCA SUMMER 1871. A similar view to the panoramic PLATE 18 but taken several years later, around the same time as PLATE 38. The main change is the recently completed Methodist Chapel on Harbour Road but there is no lifeboat station as yet. In the bottom left are a number of broad gauge wagons, all of which appear to be loaded with coal. Note the sack chute on the quayside. AUTHOR'S COLLECTION

PLATE 44: A BUSY DAY AT WATCHET TERMINUS, BY JAMES DATE, CIRCA SUMMER 1871. A lengthy passenger train passes over Goviers Lane Crossing but, sadly, the locomotive is obscured by an iron tilt wagon and it is not clear whether the ten carriages are being shunted back into the station or the train is just departing for Taunton. This number of carriages would suggest that this is likely to been one of the weekend excursions that were very popular in the early days of the line. The first known weekend excursion was in August 1862, the *West Somerset Free Press* reporting the event in great detail, including much trouble apparently with drunks! The assembled creosote tank is in place in the right foreground – this was the first version, it later being replaced with a bigger one – while work has just been completed on the construction of the Methodist Chapel. To the left of the water tank a newly installed telegraph pole supports the overhead wires. AUTHOR'S COLLECTION

PLATE 44E: AN EXCURSION TRAIN. An enlargement of the excursion train, the length of it probably exceeding that of the platform at this time. Most, if not all, of the carriages are 6-wheelers, whilst one in the middle of the rake is painted in two-tone livery; the rest appear to be plain brown, the mixture of liveries perhaps suggesting that this is a weekend excursion to Watchet from the GWR. The locomotive's safety valves are venting copious amounts of steam, so it is possible that the train is about ready to depart. Watchet was a popular destination for works outings and day trips from the inland towns, coming from as far away as Bristol, whilst the newspaper advertisement for a trip to Bristol Fair on 13th February 1872, right, indicates it was also a starting point for excursions.

BRISTOL AND EXETER RAILWAY.

BRISTOL FAIR.

CHEAP EXCURSION TO BRISTOL.

ON FRIDAY, MARCH 1st, 1872, a cheap excursion train will run as under :—

Leaving	a.m.	Fare, to and fro: Covered Carriages.
Watchet ... ... at	6. 0	
Williton ... ... ,,	6.15	
Stogumber ... ... ,,	6.30	**3**s.
Crow. Heathfield ,,	6.42	
Bishop's Lydeard ,,	7. 4	

Arriving at the new excursion platform, Bristol, about 9.20 a.m., returning from the new excursion platform at 6.30 p.m.

Children under twelve years of age, half-price. No luggage allowed.

These tickets are not transferable, and are not available by any other train or for any other station.

Bristol, February 13th, 1872.　　By order.

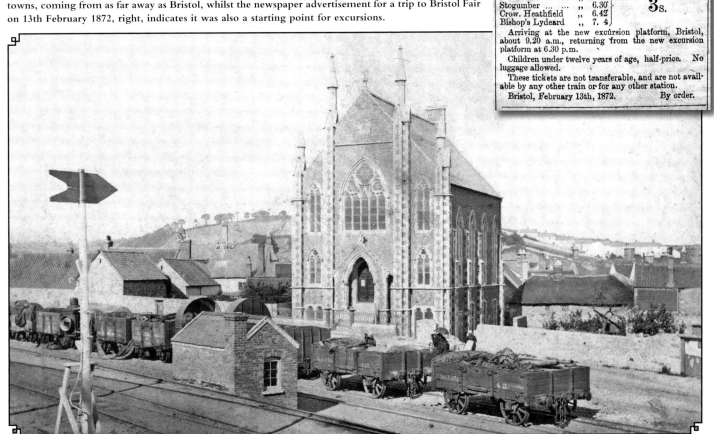

PLATE 45: THE METHODIST CHAPEL AND B&ER WAGONS IN THE GOODS YARD, BY JAMES DATE, CIRCA 1873. This photograph is of historical interest for the detail it shows of broad gauge wagons of the 1870 period but the photographer was undoubtedly more interested in the chapel. Also shown is the newly installed 'fantail' Up Starting signal on the Taunton end of the platform and the new brick building housing the weighbridge equipment. The weighbridge hut survived as an office and shelter until the 1960s, when the road was widened to make a lorry park for the docks traffic. This area is now the town car park and bus station. The two enlargements which follow overleaf show the wagons in more detail. AUTHOR'S COLLECTION

PLATE 45E-A: Two examples of B&ER 12-ton wagons, both full of scrap iron, presumably from around the dock area. B&E No. 474, nearest has one straight end and one rounded end, whilst the other, B&E No. 659, is similar but appears to have a chamfered end. Neither of these two have brakes but as they are parked on the siding that rises up to the running line, they are not in danger of running away here. Note that they have three sets of chains – coupling chains plus safety chains. The third wagon just glimpsed shows it to be a chamfered-end 7-plank open.

PLATE 45E-B: BROAD GAUGE 7-PLANK WAGONS. This second enlargement shows examples of 7-plank open wagons. All seem well used and are covered with chalked messages; the nearest again appears to be loaded with scrap metal. The shunters have made a sloppy job of the wagon sheets, as they are hanging foul of the running rails. Close study of the axlebox arrangement shows the step made by the axlebox keep. It is probable that it was this type of wagon that was involved in the fatality in 1862. The nearest wagon has a single brake block operated by a long lever. On the extreme right is the curved end of an iron tilt wagon and in the right foreground is the hut housing the weighbridge machinery.

PLATE 46. IRON ORE SHIPPING, BY JAMES DATE, CIRCA 1872. Taken from Highbank, the disc & crossbar signal stands alone, the policeman's hut having been removed to a position adjacent to Goviers Lane Crossing, in preparation for the extension works to Minehead as previously mentioned. In the foreground the capstan point lever shows up well and one of the two early steam cranes can just be seen on the far right. The western side of the harbour is full of ships, many of which will have come over from South Wales to load iron ore from the Brendon mines. This is yet another Date photograph which has previously been incorrectly attributed to H.H. Hole. SOMERSET COUNTY COUNCIL

PLATE 47: A BUSY HARBOUR, BY JAMES DATE, CIRCA 1872. Another view from what was clearly one of Date's favourite spots, around twenty sailing ships feature in the picture. This was probably a regular occurrence at this period but such numbers dwindled with the failure of the iron ore industry and gradual replacement of small wooden sailing ships by larger coastal and short sea steamers. Since this time, such numbers were only exceeded with the coming of the marina development. Note the diamond pattern of the rails on the wagon turntable. The Mineral Quay on the western side had its iron ore tippers covered over in 1873, to cut down on the noise. AUTHOR'S COLLECTION

RIGHT: PLATE 48: ENGRAVING, THE HARBOUR, WATCHET, BY J.B. & CO., UNDATED. A stylised view of the activities on the quay – photographs paint a different picture of tidiness. Shown leaving from the West Pier is a paddle steamer, which it would be impossible to identify positively from a drawing such as this but the twin masts and single smoke stack suggest that this may well be *Heather Belle* again. Engravings such as this were produced for the benefit of visitors and trippers, for resorts and towns all over the land. They were usually based on a photograph but if that were the case here, the one used for this image has yet to be found. SOMERSET COUNTY COUNCIL

LEFT: PLATE 49: THE EAST QUAY, BY JAMES DATE, CIRCA 1873. A rather fuzzy view of the East Quay, showing the later creosote tank. On the left is wood drying stack, with a horse-drawn timber tug parked next to it. Despite the rather indistinct nature of the picture, a disc & crossbar signal of the West Somerset Mineral Railway can be seen to the left, just above the town centre. AUTHOR'S COLLECTION

BELOW: PLATE 50: THE WEST SOMERSET MINERAL RAILWAY'S WATCHET TERMINUS STATION, ANONYMOUS, CIRCA 1870. Illustrating Watchet's 'other' railway and probably photographed by Date, this is the standard gauge WSMR's terminus around 1870. The tall station building faces onto the platform, beyond which the line heads across Market Street towards the Mineral Quay but the background has been blanked out. ROGER SELLICK COLLECTION

Later Period
Through Operating to Minehead
1874 to 1882

This section covers the through running to Minehead until the gauge conversion in autumn 1882.

PLATE 51: BRISTOL & EXETER RAILWAY No. 68 AT WATCHET WITH THE FIRST TRAIN FOR MINEHEAD, BY JAMES DATE, JULY 1874. Taken between 13th and 16th of July, this is a posed photograph of a special train, as indicated particularly by the document being exchanged by the two men on the platform on the right. It is now believed that this picture shows Alexander Gibson, the B&ER's Area Superintendent, accepting an authorisation to proceed from the contractor and that this was the first train to travel over the newly opened Minehead Extension – carrying railway officials, workmen and staff for the new stations – rather than being the first 'official' public train. Note the clean appearance of the engine, 4-4-0T No. 68, which was built by the Vulcan Foundry in May 1867. It had a short life, however, becoming GWR No. 2041 in 1876 but was then withdrawn in March 1880. Visible on the platform edge by the buffer beam is a large flagon of what could be cider. Note, too, the fine stone work of the platform face; it is still in place today, over 140 years later. The first carriage behind the engine is a B&ER 6-compartment Second Class with oval windows and a ventilated dog box between the compartments. Constable John Meeds poses with the engine crew of three and a number of onlookers. There appears to be a fourth engineman sitting on the platform bench and, by deduction, Henry Parker, the stationmaster, is the man standing in front of the engine. AUTHOR'S COLLECTION

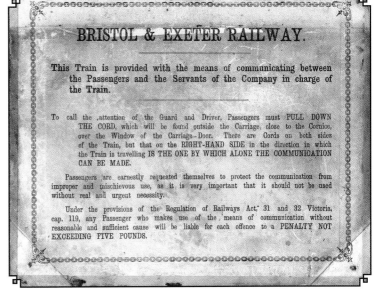

BRISTOL & EXETER RAILWAY.

This Train is provided with the means of communicating between the Passengers and the Servants of the Company in charge of the Train.

To call the attention of the Guard and Driver, Passengers must PULL DOWN THE CORD, which will be found outside the Carriage, close to the Cornice, over the Window of the Carriage-Door. There are Cords on both sides of the Train, but that on the RIGHT-HAND SIDE in the direction in which the Train is travelling IS THE ONE BY WHICH ALONE THE COMMUNICATION CAN BE MADE.

Passengers are earnestly requested themselves to protect the communication from improper and mischievous use, as it is very important that it should not be used without real and urgent necessity.

Under the provisions of the Regulation of Railways Act, 31 and 32 Victoria, cap. 119, any Passenger who makes use of the means of communication without reasonable and sufficient cause will be liable for each offence to a PENALTY NOT EXCEEDING FIVE POUNDS.

PLATE 52: LOADING SAILING SHIPS IN WATCHET HARBOUR, BY JAMES DATE, 1874-75. A nicely clear photograph showing horse-drawn carts laden with sacks of what could be grain, which are being loaded into the hold of a sailing ship by means of the sack chute. With the opening of the extension, the engine shed was moved to the new terminus at Minehead and this view is taken from its former site. In the foreground is the rubble of the recently demolished base walls which had supported the wooden structure. On the far right is the shadow cast by the water tank, which survived in place till the 1880s. According to the *West Somerset Free Press*, at around this time, on 5th December 1874, there was a fire in the storage part of the water tower, which most unfortunately destroyed stationmaster Parker's winter store of potatoes! In the right foreground, a trolley rests on the remaining section of the siding which had run into the engine shed, presumably being used to remove the rubble. In the 1980s, the site was excavated to reveal the remains of the buried foundations of the engine shed. There are two steam cranes in use; Thomas Griffiths operated the light coloured one seen in the background on the East Quay loading a railway wagon, while the darker crane was operated by Henry Hole. To the right of this crane is the larger second creosote tank. Note, too, the wire run in the foreground, partially obscured by the rubble. These wires would have connected the levers in the new signal box, provided for the opening of the extension, to the points and signals to the left of where the photographer was standing. AUTHOR'S COLLECTION

PLATE 53: THE HORSE PUMP, BY JAMES DATE, 1874-75. The site of the horse powered pump, which was used for pumping water up to the water tank between 1874 and circa 1884; it is now the garden of Seaview Terrace. The horse's rear end can just be glimpsed on the far right edge of the picture, as the animal trudged round in circles pulling the pump lever (the location of the horse pump is shown on the track plan overleaf). In the centre is the 'fantail' Starter signal and just behind the weighbridge office is a B&ER box van. AUTHOR'S COLLECTION

PLATE 54: THE GOODS YARD SIDING, HARBOUR LINE AND LIFEBOAT HOUSE, BY JAMES DATE, CIRCA 1878. The photographer was here standing on the goods yard siding, looking toward Goviers Lane Crossing. There is a worn path in the ballast, which may indicate the use of horsepower for shunting wagons up to the main line, rather than locomotives. The picture emphasizes the width of Brunel's broad gauge railway track. On the right is the newly opened lifeboat station. In 1875, a 33ft oar-powered lifeboat, named *Joseph Soames*, was stationed here and became responsible for many feats of heroism in the waters off Watchet. The author can vouch for the dangerous conditions for sailing ships, as he was involved in a rescue early in the 21st century, during a sudden storm. Many of the tales of local wrecks and rescues have been documented over the years in various books about the history of shipping and trade in the Bristol Channel. Note the wagon just seen in the goods yard on the left and the good condition of the fencing. The usual array of locals can be seen taking the sun next to the lifeboat station – they still do it today!
WEST SOMERSET PHOTO ARCHIVE

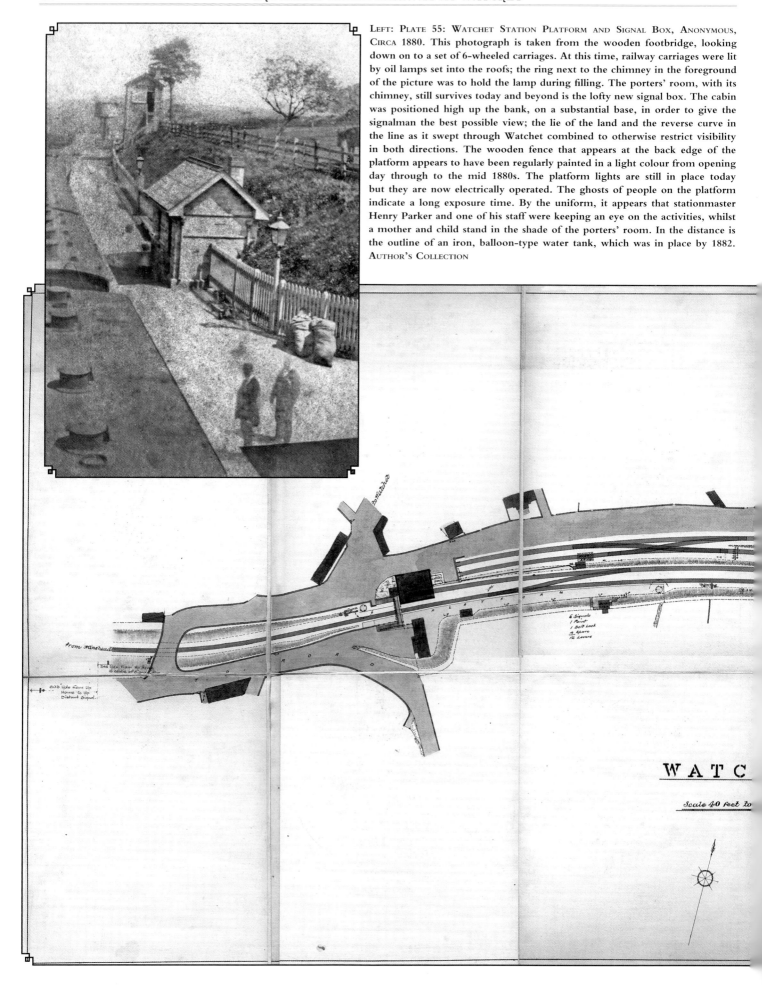

LEFT: PLATE 55: WATCHET STATION PLATFORM AND SIGNAL BOX, ANONYMOUS, CIRCA 1880. This photograph is taken from the wooden footbridge, looking down on to a set of 6-wheeled carriages. At this time, railway carriages were lit by oil lamps set into the roofs; the ring next to the chimney in the foreground of the picture was to hold the lamp during filling. The porters' room, with its chimney, still survives today and beyond is the lofty new signal box. The cabin was positioned high up the bank, on a substantial base, in order to give the signalman the best possible view; the lie of the land and the reverse curve in the line as it swept through Watchet combined to otherwise restrict visibility in both directions. The wooden fence that appears at the back edge of the platform appears to have been regularly painted in a light colour from opening day through to the mid 1880s. The platform lights are still in place today but they are now electrically operated. The ghosts of people on the platform indicate a long exposure time. By the uniform, it appears that stationmaster Henry Parker and one of his staff were keeping an eye on the activities, whilst a mother and child stand in the shade of the porters' room. In the distance is the outline of an iron, balloon-type water tank, which was in place by 1882. AUTHOR'S COLLECTION

WATC

Scale 40 feet to

RIGHT: PLATE 56E: A BRISTOL & EXETER RAILWAY BOX VAN. This enlargement from PLATE 56 on the following page provides a rare glimpse of a B&ER box van. There were several variations on this design, including cattle wagons. This example appears to be a plain box van, with a central drop down door and a shallow elliptical roof.

BELOW: WATCHET STATION TRACK PLAN, 1874-88. This is the official GWR 40 foot to 1 inch track plan for Watchet station and harbour, following opening of the Minehead Railway in 1874 and conversion to standard gauge in 1882, with additional corrections up to 1888 and stamped by the Engineer's Office at Taunton. It would appear that this plan was drawn up in 1874, to show the new layout of Watchet, which became a through station after the extension to Minehead was opened. The engine shed had been moved but the turntable and water tank were shown as still in place, along with the horse pump. Close inspection of the plan shows that these were later marked with small (red) crosses to indicate that they had been taken out; a new stop block is marked on the stub siding that led to the turntable. The East Quay siding was also moved and the wagon turntable accessing it at the station end replaced by a point. This was probably done in 1882 when the gauge was narrowed. The plan thus questions as to whether the turntable and water tower were moved to Minehead with the engine shed, as was previously thought. AUTHOR'S COLLECTION

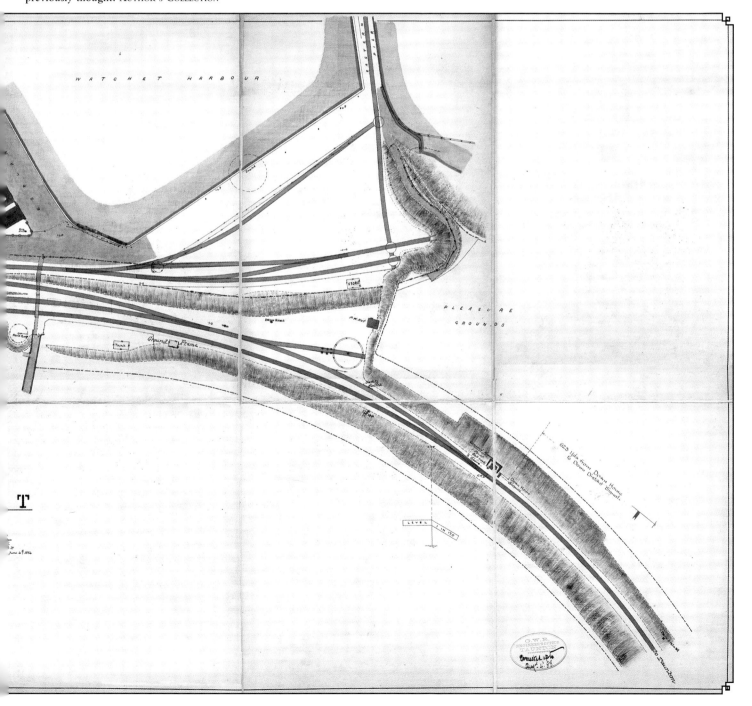

PLATE 56: THE STATION FORECOURT, JAMES DATE, CIRCA JULY 1874. The station forecourt probably soon after the extension to Minehead had opened, on 16th July 1874. The station building – that provided in 1862 – remained unaltered despite the station losing its terminus status. It was extended in 1892 with the addition of further WC facilities and an enlarged general waiting room, at which time the rear entrance seen here was walled up; ever since, passengers have had to enter the building from the platform. At some stage, possibly when this rebuilding was carried out, the original stone chimnies seen here were taken down and new ones provided in brick. As originally built, the station was identical to that at Williton, which survives intact today. The barrows in the foreground are on the pavement of South Road but what they are doing parked here is a mystery. On the left is a railway porter's hand-cart, examples of which appear, even today, on several preserved steam railways. The other barrows appear to be for fish boxes or similar goods. There is a report that, in 1867, a huge harvest of sprats were taken from the Bristol Channel. The sprat shoals usually came up the channel in the period from October to Christmas, so these could be fish porters' barrows, awaiting the next 'season'. AUTHOR'S COLLECTION

PLATE 57. WATCHET STATION FOOTBRIDGE, BY JAMES DATE, CIRCA JULY 1874. Probably taken on the same day as the previous picture, soon after the opening of the Minehead Extension. The wooden footbridge, part of the new facilities provided here, as pedestrians and passengers now had to cross over the line as it made its way west from Watchet, had a short life, being replaced with a cast iron example around 1884. The detail of the goods shed roof is also clear to see. Note the drainpipes stacked by the footbridge, which were almost certainly intended for the local drainage improvements required as a result of the Board of Trade inspector's recommendations at the time of the opening of the extension to traffic. On the left edge of the picture is the disc & crossbar Starter signal for Down trains proceeding to Washford and Minehead. Note the early train spotters on the bridge! James Date's house, Myrtle Cottage, with the thatched roof and plants growing up the walls, is prominent beyond the pipes. AUTHOR'S COLLECTION

LEFT: PLATE 58: AN ENGRAVING OF WATCHET, CIRCA 1875. This engraving may have been made to celebrate the newly opened lifeboat house on the eastern end of the esplanade. A Down train is seen entering the station from Taunton and there are a large number of wagons in the sidings; the east quay looks unusually tidy. AUTHOR'S COLLECTION

RIGHT: PLATE 59: THE HARBOUR AND EAST QUAY, BY JAMES DATE, CIRCA 1874. A well-used East Quay, with a horse and cart on the quayside and some very large logs in the foreground, probably Scandinavian pine. AUTHOR'S COLLECTION

PLATE 60: THE OLD MAN LOOKING OUT TO SEA, BY JAMES DATE, 1876–82. The final view from the broad gauge era, the branch being narrowed in October 1882. One of the steam cranes is loading a railway wagon on the right. The furthest wagon from the camera is somewhat unusual, being half an iron tilt. The nearer end is complete while the far end is cut down to 3 planks. In the centre background, the sheds covering the hydraulic tippers can be seen and the last of the elm piles have been removed from the corner of the recently widened cob. Later, a row of piles would be placed at the harbour mouth to assist in protecting ships in the harbour. The old man in the left foreground is also seen in some of James Date's other posed views of the Watchet area. He bears a strong resemblance to Daniel Nethercott, a fellow photographer and friend of Date; it is the author's opinion that the two collaborated during days out. Compare this with PLATE 20 to see the effects of some fifteen years of progress and sea erosion. AUTHOR'S COLLECTION

PLATE 61: RIGHT: MINEHEAD BEFORE THE ARRIVAL OF THE RAILWAY, ANONYMOUS, CIRCA 1865. Photographed from North Hill, little of the town and resort we know today existed then. This land is now covered with hotels, shops, houses and parks but was known to flood at this period. The station was built a few years after this picture was taken, just beyond the trees in the middle distance. The tide is out and a trading ketch is beached on the sand, unloading into a horse-drawn cart. AUTHOR'S COLLECTION

PLATE 62: BELOW: MINEHEAD AND THE RAILWAY FROM NORTH HILL, ANONYMOUS, CIRCA 1875. Shortly after opening, the railway is seen heading off top left, from the station, which was well positioned close to the beach and at the seaward end of The Avenue. The goods shed, engine shed and the Beach Family Hotel can all be made out. Considerable expansion had already taken place but a lot more was to come, with much of the land visible here being developed over the next twenty years. In the bottom left of the picture is the old quay town, with its whitewashed, thatched roof, cob cottages. AUTHOR'S COLLECTION

PLATE 63: LEFT: MINEHEAD'S NEW STATION FROM THE SEAFRONT, ANONYMOUS, CIRCA 1874. A rare previously unseen view of Minehead station, possibly in early 1874 just before completion, looking from what would later become the new seafront and Warren Road. In the right background, the first of the visitor amenities, the Beach Family Hotel, nears completion; it is still open today as the Foxes Hotel, a fully functioning facility which also provides on the job training in the hotel trade for people with learning difficulties. AUTHOR'S COLLECTION

PLATE 64: ABOVE: MINEHEAD STATION, ANONYMOUS, 1874. The station shortly after opening, with a train at the platform, including a horsebox with a train identification disk – a white diamond on a black background – hanging from the buffer beam. The goods shed is awaiting fitting of its doors, which are leant against the left side of the building. The station (similar to that still to be found at Dunster) was later extended and then completely rebuilt by the GWR. CHRIS DOWRICK COLLECTION

PLATE 65: RIGHT: MINEHEAD STATION, ANONYMOUS, 1874. A second view, probably taken on the same day, looking towards the buffer stops. In the early years, the points were worked by hand levers and note the disc & crossbar Up Starting signal. IAN COLEBY COLLECTION

PLATE 66: MINEHEAD RAILWAY STATION, ANONYMOUS, 1874. Without doubt one of the finest broad gauge railway photographs taken in west Somerset, the whole of the new Minehead Railway terminus is laid out before us here, shortly after it had opened. On the left is the newly re-erected engine shed, which had been dismantled and transported from Watchet, with a new water tank, on a timber base, next to it and a turntable positioned to the right of that. Previous thoughts that both the water tower and the turntable had also been moved here from Watchet would appear to be contradicted by the 1888 GWR track plan reproduced on pages 48–9. The 6-wheeled B&ER coach on the left is on a siding, not on the line leading into the shed. The disc & crossbar Starter signal at the end of the platform shows 'all clear', ready for the train standing in the platform to start. The points have hand levers to operate them but there are signal wires running to somewhere off picture, so there must have been a lever frame and perhaps a rudimentary cabin here; frustratingly, it does not feature in any of these views. A second 6-wheeled coach, this one in two tone livery, stands in front of the goods shed and note also the cattle pens to the right. The Beach Family Hotel is again seen nearing completion in the left background, awaiting the fitting of windows and note the man standing on the roof of the train, possibly filling or checking the compartment lights. IAN COLEBY COLLECTION

PLATE 67: A BROAD GAUGE TRAIN IN A FLOOD AT WILLITON STATION, ANONYMOUS, 24TH NOVEMBER 1877. A well-known photograph of an unidentified broad gauge B&ER 4-4-0ST standing in a flood at Williton station with a three coach Up train. It had rained heavily on the day of the picture and the stream which passes under the line here burst its banks and flooded the area. This was the afternoon train, which made it through but the evening train was not so lucky, plunging into the floodwaters in the dark and extinguishing the fire in the engine. There was a delay of nearly two hours in relighting it and the train did not arrive at Taunton until 11.00pm. The postcard from which the view was taken was published in the early years of the 20th century by Herbert Hole but it is not known who took the original photograph. The Up disc & crossbar Starter signal, at the end of the platform ramp, shows 'danger', whilst the signalman is leaning out of his box and holding a red flag – clearly unnecessarily but no doubt at the behest of the photographer. Note, too, the gangers trolley on the right. JOHN ALSOP COLLECTION

After the Broad Gauge
Post 1882

This section presents a selection of post broad gauge period views of Watchet, illustrating the immediate changes brought about by the gauge conversion

PLATE 68: LOADED WAGONS AWAITING DISPATCH, ALONGSIDE HARBOUR ROAD, ANONYMOUS, CIRCA 1899. Over the last weekend of October 1882, nearly ten years before the final abolition of the broad gauge by the Great Western Railway, the tracks of the Minehead Branch were narrowed to standard gauge – 4ft 8½ ins. The work was carried out by a workforce of 500 men, split into seven gangs of seventy working under Mr Hammett, the chief engineer of the Bristol & Exeter division of the GWR, based at Taunton, whilst the whole exercise was under the control of Mr Campfield, the District Supervisor. Here, in this early 20th century view of Harbour Road and the Methodist Chapel, the lines in the foreground can be clearly seen to be of the narrower gauge, albeit with the rails still mounted on the timber baulks that typified the broad gauge. It was to be many years yet before the whole of the baulk road was removed from the branch. The wagons are now of more modern standard gauge types, with a steel mineral wagon visible on the left of the back row. This photograph was published as a commercial picture postcard around 1905 and is therefore likely to have been the work of Herbert H. Hole. However, the photograph may have been from a plate taken a few years earlier, as the lighthouse just visible in the right background appears to be on the old pier, which would date it as prior to the 1900 storm. WEST SOMERSET PHOTO ARCHIVE

PLATE 69: A STANDARD GAUGE TRAIN IN WATCHET GOODS YARD, ANONYMOUS, CIRCA 1882-90. This previously unpublished photograph shows the standard gauge trackwork, possibly not long after the lines had been relaid. There is some evidence in the foreground of the broad gauge and there is also a quantity of track parts. Next to the brake van are the two spare baulks, which had apparently been left on the ground here since 1862. The capstan point lever can be seen to the right of the tilt wagon, whilst the Up Starter on the platform is a now a semaphore signal and a loading gauge has been provided in the exit from the goods yard. A GWR outside-framed 0-6-0ST is probably about to depart with a short goods train; the number is not quite readable but the locomotive is a '1076' Class, one of the 1581-1660 number series built between 1879 and 1881 with extended cab roofs. The yard is busy with wagons, giving an indication of the difficulties of shunting and working at this cramped and complicated site. In front of Highbank, no evidence remains of the engine shed and water tower but the tall signal box can be seen at the top of the bank. The photograph is thought to have been taken by Daniel Nethercott. AUTHOR'S COLLECTION

PLATE 70: GOVIERS LANE CROSSING, ANONYMOUS, CIRCA 1882-3. A rare view of the railway at Watchet soon after the gauge had been narrowed; the original is framed and behind glass, and had to be photographed *in situ*. The girl in the right foreground is standing by a heap of broad gauge points parts awaiting removal. On close inspection, the Up Starter signal at the end of the platform appears to still be the disc & crossbar example and is set to 'danger' or 'stop'. Goviers Lane Crossing footpath is well worn and clear to see here, passing over the lines just in front of the rake of wagons. WATCHET MARKET HOUSE MUSEUM

PLATE 71: SAILING SHIPS AT THE EASTERN ARM, BY HERBERT H. HOLE, CIRCA 1895. Several sailing ships are seen alongside the eastern arm, with the Dublin registered topsail schooner *Emma Ernest* moored to the quay in the right foreground. A regular caller at Watchet, she was built at Milford Haven in 1876 and re-registered at Faversham in 1900. Sold out of trade in 1929, she was then bought for use as a clubhouse by World Explorers Ltd in 1933, moored on the Thames at Charing Cross Pier. Severely damaged by a bomb blast in the Second World War, she was broken up in 1946. It is noticeable that there are fewer ships in the harbour; by this date, the iron ore trade had ceased and coal deliveries were declining. The timber pile extension to the western arm was in place from 1887 till the great storm of 1900. Note one of the steam cranes in action unloading another unidentified topsail schooner; the author remembers both of the steam cranes parked, derelict, on the quay in the early 1950s. Incidentally, the three timber stakes sunk into the harbour floor were to aid in warping ships away from the quay prior to setting sail. AUTHOR'S COLLECTION

PLATE 72. DISMANTLING OF THE MINERAL QUAY EQUIPMENT, ANONYMOUS, CIRCA 1887-1900. An almost deserted harbour, with one of the steam cranes positioned on the Mineral Quay apparently dismantling the remains of the iron ore unloading equipment. In the late 1880s, competition from cheaper and better quality imported iron ore caused the demise of mining on the Brendon Hills. A revival in the early 20th century met with no success and had foundered within a few years; the full history of the mining industry of the area and the railway which served it is given in M.H. Jones book *The Brendon Hills Iron Mines and the West Somerset Mineral Railway*. On the quayside on the left is the ballast mountain left over from incoming sailing ships; early maps of Watchet show a 'ballast island' near the harbour mouth, where unwanted stones were dumped overboard previously by incoming ships just before entering. In front of this are bundles of what is likely to be rags or wood pulp destined for Watchet paper mill. The steam crane on the eastern pier was still broad gauge and was running on a short length of broad gauge track left *in situ*. The impending storm on the eve of the new century was to smash most of the wooden pier forming the western arm and to severely damage the Mineral Quay. This was subsequently demolished leaving the western arm much as we see it today, some 100 years later. AUTHOR'S COLLECTION

PLATE 73. SAILING SHIPS LOADING FLOUR AT WATCHET, ANONYMOUS, CIRCA 1895. The sack chute is in full view here, loading the hold. The flour was ground in the water powered corn mills located in the town, the largest of which was at work until it burnt down in 1911. As with many of these pictures, the names of the vessels were not recorded but that of the ketch in the foreground may yet be determined; although partially obscured, it can be discerned that the ship was registered here at Watchet. SOMERSET COUNTY COUNCIL

PLATE 74: WATCHET REGATTA, ANONYMOUS, 1890. A regatta underway at the harbour in 1890, complete with marquee, flagpole and Union Jack flag, and crowds of watchers all around the steam cranes and on the sidings. Note that whilst the steam crane on the eastern pier was initially left as broad gauge with its own length of track, the nearer one had been converted to run on the standard gauge line along the quay. WATCHET MARKET HOUSE MUSEUM

PLATE 75: WATCHET HARBOUR AFTER THE GREAT STORM OF 1900, ANONYMOUS, JANUARY 1901. This view is looking north west across the harbour, showing how exposed the inner dock was following the devastating damage caused by the great storm a few weeks earlier, much of the northern quay having been swept away. A rake of sheeted GWR open wagons occupy the siding in the foreground, with another sheeted open, a low sided wagon and a box van on the siding behind. Note the stump of the Mineral Quay in the left background. The photograph is likely to have been taken by Herbert H. Hole. M.H. JONES COLLECTION

Appendix 1

A Selection of Stereograph Cards

LEFT: Mortar production underway for the eastern quay wall in 1861, with the western Mineral Quay in the right background (see PLATE 2). JOHN HANNAVY COLLECTION

RIGHT: A general view of the earthworks and site leveling for the station and goods yard in 1861; note all horse and man power (see PLATE 3). The use of a stereo viewer is recommended to show off the properties of these photographs and modern stereo viewers are readily available on the internet from a few pounds. JOHN HANNAVY COLLECTION

LEFT: Again in 1861, this view is from the cliff top looking down on the construction of the eastern quay and arm. The timber framing is awaiting fill with stone (see PLATE 4). JOHN HANNAVY COLLECTION

Appendix 2
Brief Biography of the Author and Select Bibliography

The author has been a regular visitor to Watchet since 1953 – Coronation year – for the family annual holiday. From the outset, he explored the railway system in the area, still exclusively steam worked at that date, and watched the cargo ships that arrived at the harbour loaded with coal from South Wales, paper pulp from the Baltic and esparto grass from Africa for banknote manufacture.

Since 1960, he has been a volunteer on the Bluebell Railway in Sussex, where he has recently served as a Trustee on the management committee, with oversight of the Standards of Preservation. A long term member of the Broad Gauge Society, he has been able to call on the expertise and help of its members in the production of this book. Their website gives details of the benefits of membership (www. broadgauge.org.uk).

Should anyone reading this book wish to correct any errors that might have occurred or have further images that they would like to share, please do not hesitate to contact the author via the publishers.

The following is a brief list of books consulted during the compilation of the captions for this volume and also suggested further reading:

The Brendon Hills Iron Mines and the West Somerset Mineral Railway, M.H. Jones, Lightmoor Press 2011
The Minehead Branch, Ian Coleby, Lightmoor Press 2nd Ed. 2011
Closing Down Sail, W. Martin Benn, privately pub'd, 2011
West Country Passenger Steamers, Grahame Farr, T. Stephenson & Sons Ltd, 1967
The Locomotives of the Great Western Railway, Parts 2 & 5, The Railway Correspondence & Travel Society, 1952 & 1958

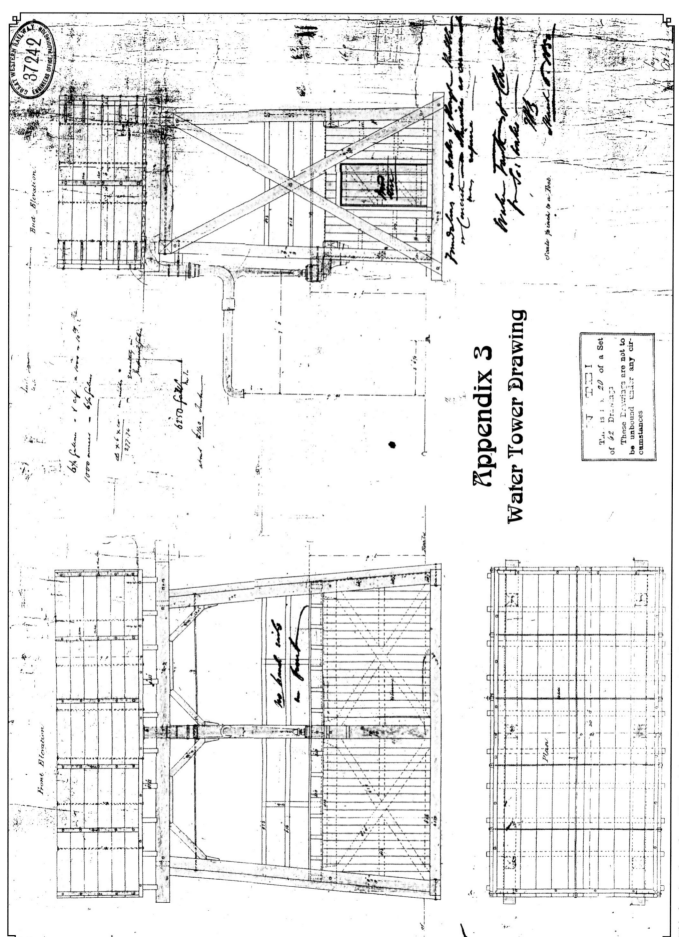

Appendix 3
Water Tower Drawing

This drawing dates from 1850 and shows the construction of a typical wood framed water tower, identical to that used at Watchet between 1862 and 1884. In the closed in store on the ground floor was kept fire lighting wood – and the station master's potatoes! The first floor deck was used for coal and in the Watchet version, this was boarded in to keep the weather off the fuel and the staff. One of the written notes indicates that the capacity of the tank was 6,250 gallons. Other examples of this standard pattern could be found all over the west of England and in South Wales.